38-297

EAGLES, HAWKS, and OWLS

A GOLDEN JUNIOR GUIDE®

EAGLES, HAWKS, and OWLS

By Alvin, Virginia, and Robert Silverstein
Illustrated by Kristin Kest

Consultant: Paul Lehman, field ornithologist and editor of *Birding* Magazine

A GOLDEN BOOK • NEW YORK
Western Publishing Company, Inc., Racine, Wisconsin 53404

Eagles, Hawks, and Owls

are all *birds of prey*. Birds of prey can be found all over the world. Some live on freezing mountaintops. Others live in steamy jungles. A few live among people in crowded cities. Birds of prey are often called *raptors,* from the Latin word for "one who takes by force." All raptors are meat eaters, and most are skilled hunters. Some birds of prey, such as eagles and hawks, hunt during the day. Owls hunt mostly at night. In this book, you will meet some of the most familiar or unusual birds of prey.

Scops Owl

flight muscles

third eyelid

eye

beak

Raptors have a third eyelid that protects the eye during flight and when capturing prey.

Raptors often swallow their prey whole. Or they may tear apart their food, using their sharp, powerful beak.

A Raptor's feet have four toes, with sharp claws called *talons.* Talons are used to kill prey and carry it away.

toe

talon

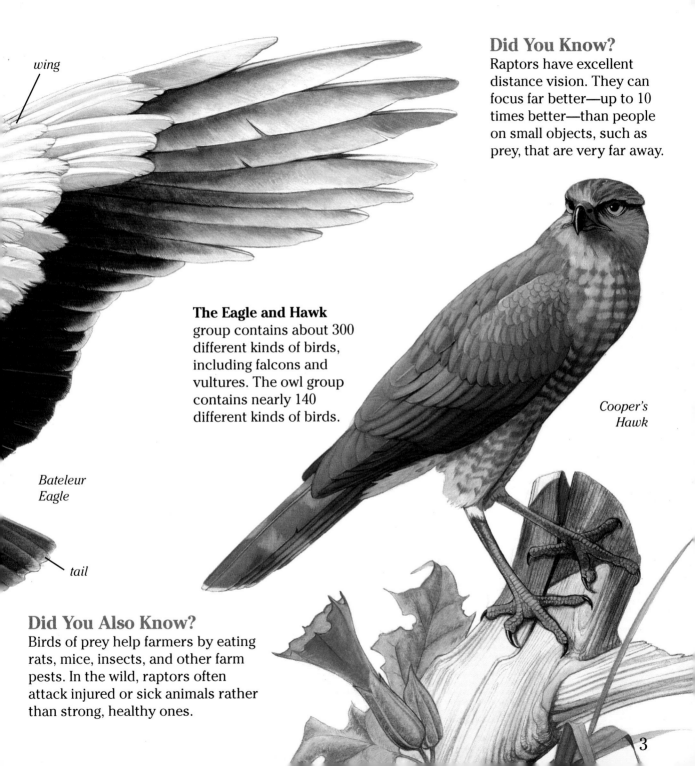

wing

Did You Know?

Raptors have excellent distance vision. They can focus far better—up to 10 times better—than people on small objects, such as prey, that are very far away.

The Eagle and Hawk group contains about 300 different kinds of birds, including falcons and vultures. The owl group contains nearly 140 different kinds of birds.

Cooper's Hawk

Bateleur Eagle

tail

Did You Also Know?

Birds of prey help farmers by eating rats, mice, insects, and other farm pests. In the wild, raptors often attack injured or sick animals rather than strong, healthy ones.

3

All Birds of Prey

are alike in some ways, but there are many differences between them. Some of the ways used to tell them apart are given below. Falcons, because they are so closely related to hawks, are usually considered hawks. But they have some unique features of their own. Vultures are close relatives, too. You will learn more about all these birds of prey later in this book.

Eagles

- ❑ Eagles soar, hardly flapping their broad wings.
- ❑ Eagles have a tail spread like a fan.
- ❑ Eagles have large toes and powerful talons.
- ❑ Eagles have a large, hooked beak.
- ❑ Eagles make huge nests from sticks.
- ❑ Eagles lay 1 or 2 pointed eggs. Most are white, but some have spots or speckles.

Bald Eagle

wing

beak

foot

Did You Know?

Most raptor females are a lot larger and stronger than their mates.

4

Hawks

- ❏ Many hawks fly fast and low, rapidly flapping their rounded wings.
- ❏ Many hawks have a long tail.
- ❏ Hawks have long, narrow toes and talons.
- ❏ Hawks have a short, hooked beak.
- ❏ Hawks often use nests built by other birds, rather than build their own nests.
- ❏ Hawks lay 3 to 5 pointed, spotted eggs.

Red-tailed Hawk

beak

wing

wing

foot

Great Horned Owl

Owls

- ❏ Owls swoop down silently from a perch, using broad wings with soft, fluffy feathers on the edges.
- ❏ Most owls have a rounded tail.
- ❏ Most owls have small, delicate toes and talons.
- ❏ Owls have a small, hooked beak, partly covered by feathers.
- ❏ Many kinds of owls build nests in tree holes.
- ❏ Owls lay 2 to 6 round white eggs.

beak

foot

Great Horned Owl egg

Peregrine Falcon egg

Turkey Vulture egg

5

Eagles are found all over the world. They are a symbol of freedom and power as they soar gracefully through the air, going for hours without flapping their wings. Most eagles spend a lot of time sitting almost motionless on a perch, keeping a careful eye out for any animals moving below.

Eagles build their huge stick nests high up in trees or on remote cliffs. They add to the nest every year. A very old nest can be 10 feet wide, 20 feet deep, and weigh over 6,000 pounds—the size of two compact cars!

Did You Know?
Eagle and other raptor chicks are born covered with a soft, warm fluff called *down.* After a few weeks, real feathers start to grow in.

Bald Eagle

female with young

Did You Also Know?

Some eagles, such as the Short-toed Eagle that lives in Africa, are expert snake catchers. Snakes can be very dangerous prey!

male

Harpy Eagle

Harpy Eagles, which are found in Central and South America, are named after the ferocious monster—half bird, half woman—in Greek mythology. These 3-foot-long eagles swoop down into the rainforests to catch monkeys, sloths, and large birds such as parrots.

7

Golden Eagles

Golden Eagles are one of only two kinds of North American eagle. They grow to 3 feet long, not including their tail, and have a wingspan of about 7 feet. Most other eagles are smaller. Hawk Eagles of Africa and Asia, for example, are only 1½ to 2 feet long. The Golden Eagle hunts rabbits, squirrels, and other birds, but it may also eat young lambs or deer. It has been called the "king of birds" because it is such a mighty hunter.

The Adult Golden Eagle's neck is covered with golden-brown feathers, which can be hard to see from far away.

Golden Eagle

male

8

Did You Know?
Eagles mate for life. Unlike most other raptors, male and female eagles take turns sitting on the eggs, and both feed and care for the young.

soaring flight silhouette

female

head-on flight silhouette

The Golden Eagle, with its large brown eyes, can spot a rabbit from up to 2 miles away. It can then dive down to catch the fleeing rabbit at speeds of 150 to 200 miles per hour!

Did You Also Know?
The American Indians highly prize Golden Eagle feathers, which they once used for their ceremonial headdresses.

9

Bald Eagles

Bald Eagles are the only other North American eagles. Like Golden Eagles, they are about 3 feet long. They catch fish and small birds along rivers, lakes, and seashores and will even eat animals that are already dead. Most Bald Eagles are found in Alaska. Bald Eagles are not really bald—they just look that way from a distance because their heads are covered with white feathers.

male Bald Eagle

Bald Eagles don't always catch their own fish. They will also steal it from other fishing birds such as this osprey.

Steller's Sea Eagle

Other Sea Eagles include the huge brown-and-white Steller's Sea Eagle, which is almost 4 feet long and has a wingspan of 8 feet.

adult Bald Eagle

juvenile Bald Eagle

Did You Know?
The Bald Eagle was chosen as the national bird of the United States in 1782.

Young Bald Eagles have brown heads. The white head feathers do not grow in until the bird reaches 4 or 5 years of age.

11

Hawks are superb hunters. They have the best eyesight of any animal. With their large, light-colored eyes, they can spot even tiny prey at great distances. Hawks range in size from about 10 inches to 2 feet. Their long tail helps them steer and quickly change direction while flying. Sailing close to the ground, the hawk matches every move of its fleeing prey. There are three main groups, or families, of North American hawk. You will discover more about birds belonging to each of these groups in the pages that follow.

The Red-shouldered Hawk will return to the same territory year after year, usually an open woodland near a river, stream, or swamp. It often decorates its nest with webs spun by tent caterpillars.

Red-shouldered Hawk

The Sharp-shinned Hawk, at only 1 foot long, is still a fierce hunter. It eats mainly small birds. Before eating its prey, it perches on a branch or stump and plucks out the small bird's feathers.

Did You Know?
Most hawks put on lively aerial displays over their home territories, soaring, flapping, and diving. The male and female will sometimes fly together, holding on to each other's talons while tumbling through the air.

Sharp-shinned Hawk

Did You Also Know?
In the fall, at Hawk Mountain in Pennsylvania, numerous Sharp-shinned Hawks can be seen passing overhead as they migrate south for the winter.

13

Red-tailed Hawks

are the most common hawks in North America. Like eagles, hawks in this family can soar for hours. They glide on air currents, beating their wings only once in a while. Red-tailed Hawks build large, bowl-shaped nests out of sticks on a cliff or the top of a tall tree. Hawks are sometimes mistakenly called *buzzards.* For example, the Rough-legged Hawk, another often-seen bird in North America, is also known as the Rough-legged Buzzard.

The Red-tailed Hawk, which lives in woodlands and open country, eats mainly rabbits and rodents. Like other hawks, the Red-tailed Hawk often swallows its prey whole.

Red-tailed Hawk

The Roadside Hawk of Mexico and South America perches on fence posts or wires by the roadside, watching for lizards, scorpions, and insects.

Roadside Hawk

Did You Know?
Some male and female hawks are about the same size and have the same colors and markings. This is very unusual for a bird of prey.

Goshawks are often called *Chicken Hawks* because they will sometimes steal chickens from farms. Goshawks (pronounced GOSS-hawks) are large, swift, aggressive, and fearless. In pursuit of a meal, they will even chase prey on foot! They live in forests all around the world and hunt birds, squirrels, and sometimes foxes.

Northern Goshawk

The Northern Goshawk is found in North America, Europe, and Asia. Its feathers are soft and gooselike.

16

The White Goshawk of Australia is a striking bird, with snow-white feathers, a black beak, and ruby-red eyes.

Did You Know?
Goshawk couples often have a favorite food. For example, one pair may eat only game birds such as grouse, while another may eat only crows.

White Goshawk

Did You Also Know?
Goshawks belong to a group known as *accipiters,* which are hawks that live in deeply wooded areas. As a group, accipiters are quite secretive and are seen less often than most other hawks.

17

Northern Harriers

Northern Harriers are also known as *Marsh Hawks*. They fly over wetlands, open marshes, and meadows, looking for mice, frogs, snakes, small birds, and insects to eat. Up to 2 feet in length, Northern Harriers are found throughout most of the world. Adult males are bluish gray. Females and young birds are brown. All the birds in this family have owl-like faces and long legs.

male

Northern Harrier

female

Did You Know?
Some male harriers have two or three mates at a time. They have to work very hard to feed all those nests full of chicks!

The Female Northern Harrier builds her nest on the ground in marshy areas. She sits on the eggs all by herself. The male brings her food and feeds the young when they hatch.

18

Kites are close relatives of hawks. Most kinds swoop gracefully in circles overhead, using their long, pointed wings and forked tail. Then they sail down, or drop down feet first, and hover over the ground, looking for prey such as frogs, snakes, insects, or rodents. Kites are found on every continent except Antarctica. Some have unusual feeding habits. The Snail Kite, found in Florida, eats only apple snails! Kites sometimes nest and hunt together in small groups.

The American Swallow-tailed Kite of the southern United States is 2 feet long and has a scissorlike tail. The bird skims the water's surface to drink and bathe.

American Swallow-tailed Kite

Did You Know?
Fish-eating ospreys are closely related to hawks. Once endangered, ospreys are now making a comeback.

Falcons are some of the world's fastest fliers. There are many different kinds of falcons, some quite small. The Merlin is even called a *Pigeon Hawk* because of its size. The gyrfalcons, the largest birds in this group, are nearly 2 feet long. Falcons don't build nests. They borrow empty nests or lay their eggs in a hole in a tree, on a cliff ledge, or even on the ground. Some falcons like to make their homes on top of church towers or other tall buildings.

American Kestrel

The American Kestrel, at 10 inches, is the smallest and most common falcon in North America. In Europe the Kestrel is often called the *Windhover* because of how it hovers in midair, flapping its wings against the wind. It eats insects and small rodents.

Black Vulture

The Crested Caracara, although not a true falcon, is a very close relative. Found mainly in Central and South America, it can run fast and is aggressive. The Caracara will march right up to the catch of a big vulture and grab it away.

Crested Caracara

Did You Know?

A falcon uses its feet to knock live prey—most often other birds—to the ground. But unlike most raptors, it does not kill with its feet. It uses its beak, which has toothlike points, to crush the neck of the stunned prey.

21

Peregrine Falcons

Peregrine Falcons make breathtaking dives. With wings swept back, they swoop down to attack prey, using their sharp claws. Peregrines are about 1½ feet long. They can be identified by a dark "mustache" mark on the cheeks. Once very common, Peregrines had almost disappeared from many parts of the world by the 1970s, but special breeding and release programs were set up. Today Peregrines can be found in a few large cities, nesting high up on rooftops, the steel supports of bridges, and even skyscraper ledges.

Peregrine Falcon

Peregrine Falcons are the birds most often used today in the art of falconry. Training birds of prey to hunt in cooperation with people began over 3,000 years ago in China and Persia and is still practiced today, but mostly to demonstrate the birds' amazing skills.

When a Peregrine spots its prey, the high-speed chase begins. But no other bird can outfly it. Peregrines like to eat ducks and other swimming birds, which is why they are often called *Duck Hawks.*

Peregrine chasing a duck

Prairie Falcons are closely related to Peregrines but are lighter in color and are found mainly on open plains.

Prairie Falcon

Did You Know?
Raptors that are endangered as a result of pesticide poisoning, hunting, and habitat loss are now protected by law.

23

Vultures

Vultures may seem ugly close up, but they are beautiful in flight. Found on almost all continents, they soar with their wings spread out wide. Most have no feathers on their head. This allows them to eat some very messy things without getting too messy themselves! Vultures feed on dead animals that would spread disease if left to rot. The Lammergeier, a close relative of vultures, often eats the bones of a carcass after vultures are done with it. It carries them high up in the air, then drops them onto rocks to break them into easy-to-eat pieces.

Turkey Vultures

Turkey Vultures, found in North America, have a red wrinkled head, like a turkey's. They circle around in the air looking for food. If one spots a dead animal, it drops to the ground. Others nearby soon follow it down.

Did You Know?

People think owls are wise because their heads and faces are more human-looking than those of most other birds. But actually, many other birds are smarter than owls.

Owls have the best hearing of any bird. But those tufts of feathers on their head, which look like ears, are not ears. They are just there for decoration. Their *real* ears are hidden under their feathers!

Long-eared Owl

ear tuft

Here is a peek at the real ear.

Did You Also Know?

Owls can see clearly by day and even better at night. But they cannot shift their eyes to look at things, as people do. Instead, they must turn their head— which goes almost all the way around!

27

Great Horned Owls

Great Horned Owls are often called "tigers of the air" because of their large size, deep, loud voice, and bright eyes. Small animals may be frightened by their nightly hooting. Also often called a *Cat Owl* because of its catlike face, the Great Horned Owl can grow to 2 feet long, but it is not the largest owl. The Great Gray Owl of Canada and Alaska is 2½ feet long. Great Horned Owls have a white "collar" around their throat and can be found in many different places, including North American forests and canyons. Males and females take turns sitting on the eggs.

Great Horned Owl

Great Horned Owls will chase and eat skunks regularly. The unpleasant odor doesn't seem to bother them.

Did You Know?

An owl's mouth may look small, but it can open wide enough to swallow even large prey whole.

Screech Owls

Screech Owls are named for their call, a trembling whistle that can go up and down the scale. The call of the Eastern Screech Owl sounds more like the whinnying of a horse than a screech. Some people think that hearing this call is bad luck. Screech Owls are the most common owls in North America. You can often find their nests near the edges of cities and suburbs. They eat a wide variety of prey, including small rodents, frogs, and fish. In summer, they eat large numbers of insects.

Screech Owls are just 8 to 12 inches long. They are the only small owls with ear tufts.

Eastern Screech Owls

Did You Know?
Eastern Screech Owls have all red or all gray feathers. When red and gray owls mate, some of their babies are red while the others are gray.

Barn Owls and Bay Owls

Barn Owls and Bay Owls are found around the world. They form a separate family from all other owls. About 1½ feet long, Barn Owls like to live in old churches or empty houses. If you startle them, they will fly out, sometimes making eerie shrieks. Their body is mostly orange-brown, with brownish and white spots. Bay Owls, found in Asia, are close relatives of Barn Owls but have tiny ear tufts. Barn and Bay Owls eat mice and rats. Dutch farmers even build special doors to let these useful birds get in and out of their barns easily.

Barn Owl

ear tuft

face of Short-eared Owl

face of Bay Owl

Barn and Bay Owls look as if they have heart-shaped faces. This is because of how their feathers are arranged. Also, the eyes of Barn and Bay Owls are smaller and darker than those of most other owls.

Barn Owls, like most other owls, have soft, fluffy feathers at the edges of their wings to muffle any flapping sounds. Their white underparts and silent flight make them seem ghostly as they fly overhead.

Did You Know?
Barn Owls don't hoot, but they make a loud screech, hiss, and snap their beak. Bay Owls usually call with a single soft hoot.

31

Burrowing Owls

usually live underground in burrows dug by snakes, prairie dogs, or gophers. A half dozen or more pairs may live together. (Most other owls either live alone or live in pairs.) Burrowing Owls have very long legs and can get around on the ground quite well. They hunt both day and night and eat young prairie dogs, rabbits, chipmunks, bats, and insects.

Burrowing Owls may often be seen during the day sitting in front of their burrow, watching for prey.

Burrowing Owls

Did You Know?
Young Burrowing Owls often fool predators by hissing like a rattlesnake.

32

Barred Owls have dark eyes. They are about 2 feet long and have no ear tufts. Brownish gray bars run across their undersides. These owls, which are common in the Deep South, are often called "hoot owls." Some Southerners claim that the Barred Owl's eight-note call asks, "Who COOKS for YOU? Who COOKS for y'all?" Barred Owls can also be found in colder regions, such as the Northeast and central Canada.

Barred Owl

Barred Owls are shy and rarely come out of their wooded swamps or forests. They nest in tree cavities. Like all birds of prey, they must eat large amounts of food to stay warm in winter.

Did You Know?
Spotted Owls, found mostly in the Pacific Northwest, are close relatives of Barred Owls. Some people want to stop loggers from cutting down the forests where these owls live, since they are the endangered birds' last refuge.

33

Elf Owls and Pygmy Owls

are the smallest of all the owls. Elf Owls are less than 6 inches long. They live in deserts in the southwestern United States and in Mexico, often nesting in holes woodpeckers have bored into the giant Saguaro cactus. Pygmy Owls, found in North and South America, are related to Elf Owls but are a little larger, about 7 inches long, and their tails are longer. In Africa and Asia, Pygmy Owls are called *Owlets*.

Elf Owl

Pygmy Owls eat mainly birds, mice, and young squirrels—animals that are often even bigger than they are.

Pygmy Owl

Did You Know?
Unlike most owls, Pygmy Owls will hunt during either the day or the night.

Male Elf Owls sing from inside their nest hole to attract females. When a male wins a mate, he feeds her until their babies are half-grown.

34

Snowy Owls are almost entirely covered with thick white feathers. Even their feet look as if they are wearing fur boots. This helps the owls blend in with the snow in northern Canada and the Arctic, where they live. The feathers on the feet also protect against frostbite. Every few years, these 2-foot-long owls appear in large numbers in southern Canada and the northern United States, searching for food. This is because their usual prey, rodents called *lemmings,* have temporarily become scarce.

Female Snowy Owls have dark brown spots or bands that help to hide them when they are sitting on their nests among the rocks. The males are almost pure white.

Snowy Owl

male

female

Did You Know?
Most owls have feathers with colors and patterns that make them hard for predators to see when they are perched on a tree or rock ledge.

For Further Reading

With this book, you've only just begun to explore some exciting new worlds. Why not continue to learn about the wonderful creatures known as eagles, hawks, and owls? For example, you might browse through *Birds* and *Bird Life* (both *Golden Guides*), which contain many details about the species in this book and others. Other Golden Books you might enjoy are *Birds* by Mary Packard and the *Big Golden Book of Backyard Birds.* Finally, be sure to visit your local library, where you will discover a variety of titles on the subject.